Their Daughter, My Baby

I Miss You Every Day

Maria Suggett

Balboa Press books may be ordered through booksellers or by contacting:

Balboa Press
A Division of Hay House
1663 Liberty Drive
Bloomington, IN 47403
www.balboapress.com
844-682-1282

Because of the dynamic nature of the Internet, any web addresses or links contained in this book may have changed since publication and may no longer be valid. The views expressed in this work are solely those of the author and do not necessarily reflect the views of the publisher, and the publisher hereby disclaims any responsibility for them.

Any people depicted in stock imagery provided by Getty Images are models, and such images are being used for illustrative purposes only.
Certain stock imagery © Getty Images.

ISBN: 979-8-7652-3540-9 (sc)
ISBN: 979-8-7652-3541-6 (e)

Library of Congress Control Number: 2022918881

Print information available on the last page.

Balboa Press rev. date: 10/15/2022

Their Daughter, My Baby

Ever since I was a little girl, I always wanted to be a mommy. I had six younger brothers and sisters and I loved being part of a big family. I thought being a mommy would be the best feeling in the world.

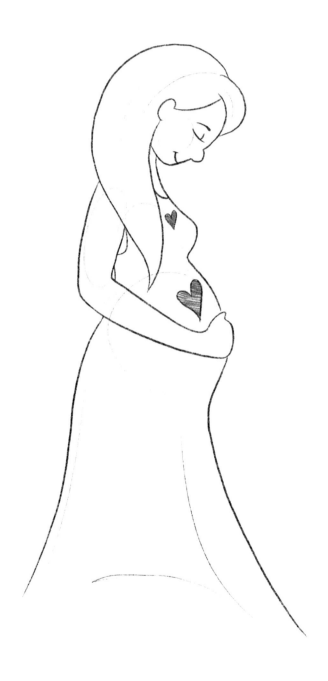

When I found out you were growing inside me, I was so happy. I dreamed of the wonderful life we would have.

But I was young. I knew how to be a big sister, but I did not know how to be a mommy. I knew that you should have a better life than I could give you.

I decided to let you be part of a new family that could take better care of you. That is how much I loved you. It was not a decision I liked, because it would mean that I would not get to be with you, but I decided it was the best thing for you so that you could have a good life.

While you were still growing inside me, a woman and her husband were wishing for a new baby in their family to love and care for. When they heard about you from the woman who was helping me find a family, they asked if they could keep you for their own after you were born. I said yes.

On the day you were born I did not see you. Your new parents picked you up from the hospital and you became their baby. They were so in love with you.

I was very happy for you and your new parents, but I was very sad in my heart. I knew you were part of the best family you could be with, but I missed you.

I had a hole in my heart where your heart had been growing inside me. I missed you every day.

I was so happy to know that you were living nearby with your new family, and that they were taking good care of you. You never felt far away from me, and that was a wonderful feeling. The hole in my heart slowly started to fill. I missed you every day.

As you grew into an adorable little girl, I received lots of cards and letters from your adoptive parents. They always said thank you for the special gift in their lives – and that gift was you.

One day I met your parents. They smiled kindly at me and said that you looked like me. They gave me one of your school pictures. Though I never saw them again, it was one of the best days in my life. My heart filled up a lot that day.

It made me happy to know how much they loved you. I still missed you every day. My heart filled up more and more.

The first time I saw you, you were a teenager. It was also the first time you met your birth father and grandparents. It was a big day for all of us.

You were amazing on that day. You made everyone feel special and loved. I know it was because you had been raised by a wonderful family. I was so proud of you.

When you grew into a young woman, you married a wonderful, handsome man.

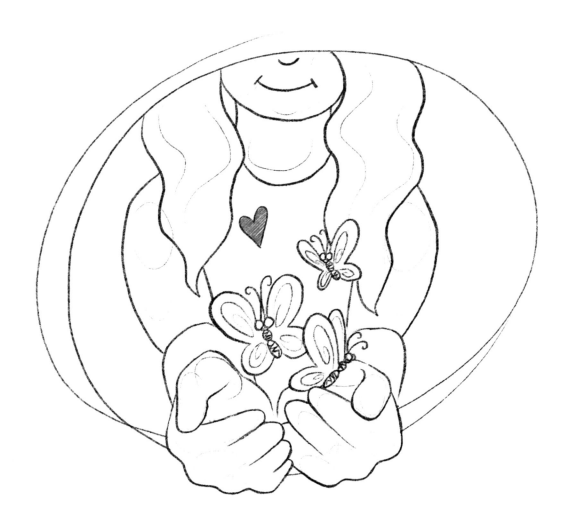

You were not able to have children of your own, so you and your husband adopted three baby boys and became a family.

As you grew older and lived far away from me, I was sad that I might lose touch with you forever. I missed you every day.

I did not want that to happen, so I moved closer to you hoping to be part of your life. We started to see each other often. It was so nice.

Since you were born, I kept a pink folder with all the cards, letters, and pictures I had received from your adopted family. I gave it to you to show you that I was never far away from you in my heart, and how much I always loved you. I missed you every day.

You and I had some long talks about when you were born and why I gave you up for adoption. It was hard to explain that because I loved you, I let another family take care of you. You adopted three boys who needed you, so you understood why adoption is a good thing, even though it is hard sometimes. You thanked me for giving you a great life and it filled my heart completely.

After that, we spent more and more time together. We became more of a family. And that is how we are now – a real family. My heart continues to stay full.

You were and will always be part of my life. You know that now. I am so happy to have a chance to be part of your life. My heart is full and happy. I love you forever.

Printed in the United States
by Baker & Taylor Publisher Services